**CUTE & EASY**

# Princesses, Fairies & Ballerinas!

# Cute & Easy Cake Toppers
## for any Princess Party or Girly Celebration!

# Contributors

Amanda Mumbray

Following a career in finance, Amanda Mumbray launched her cake business in 2010 and has gone from strength to strength, delighting customers with her unique bespoke creations and winning several Gold medals at various International Cake Shows. Amanda's **Clever Little Cupcake** company is based near Manchester, UK:
www.cleverlittlecupcake.co.uk

Elina Prawito

Elina Prawito is a cake designer based in Auckland, New Zealand. Her passion for cake design started when she made her son's 1st birthday cake in 2007 and fell in love with sugar art and cake design. 3 years later **bake-a-boo cakes** was born! You can view more of Elina's stunning work at:
**www.bakeaboo.com**

Helen Penman

Helen Penman has been designing cakes for over 15 years and her work has been featured in a wide range of cake books and magazines. She has also written several cake decorating and modelling books of her own, and runs a successful cake company from her home in Kent, UK.
www.toonicetoslice.co.uk

Lesley Grainger

Lesley Grainger has been imaginative since birth and has baked since she was old enough to hold a spatula. When life-saving surgery prompted a radical rethink, Lesley left a successful corporate career to pursue her passion for cake making. Lesley is based in Greenock, Scotland. Say 'hello' at:
**www.lesleybakescakes.co.uk**

First published in 2014 by Kyle Craig Publishing

Text and illustration copyright © 2014 Kyle Craig Publishing

Editor: Alison McNicol

Design: Julie Anson

ISBN: 978-1-908-707-40-6

A CIP record for this book is available from the British Library.

A Kyle Craig Publication

www.kyle-craig.com

# Contents

# Welcome!

Welcome to '**Princesses, Fairies & Ballerinas**', the latest title in the **Cute & Easy Cake Toppers Collection**.

Each book in the series focuses on a specific theme, and here we have compiled a gorgeous selection of beautiful cake toppers that will delight any budding ballerinas, pretty princesses or fabulous little fairies!

Whether you're an absolute beginner or an accomplished cake decorator, these projects are suitable for all skill levels, and we're sure that you will have as much fun making them as we did!

Enjoy!

## Fondant/Sugarpaste/Gumpaste

**Fondant/Sugarpaste** – Ready-made fondant, also called ready to roll icing, is widely available in a selection of fantastic colours. Most regular cake decorators find it cheaper to buy a larger quantity in white and mix their own colours using colouring pastes or gels. Fondant is used to cover entire cakes, and as a base to make modelling paste for modelling and figures (see below).

**Modelling Paste** – Used throughout this book. Firm but pliable and dries faster and harder than fondant/sugarpaste. When making models, fondant can be too soft so we add CMC/Tylose powder to thicken it.

**Gumpaste** – Also known as 'Florist Paste'. More pliable than fondant, but dries very quickly and becomes quite hard, so it is widely used for items like flowers that are delicate but need to hold their shape when dry. Gumpaste can be made by adding Gum-Tex/Gum Tragacanth to regular fondant.

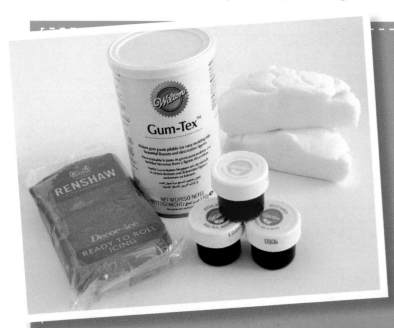

## How to Make Modelling Paste

Throughout this book we refer to 'paste', meaning modelling paste. You can convert regular shop-bought fondant into modelling paste by adding CMC/Tylose powder, which is a thickening agent.

Add approx 1 tsp of CMC/Tylose powder to 225g (8oz) of fondant/sugarpaste. Knead well and leave in an airtight freezer bag for a couple of hours.

Add too much and it will crack. If this happens, add in a little shortening (white vegetable fat) to make it pliable again.

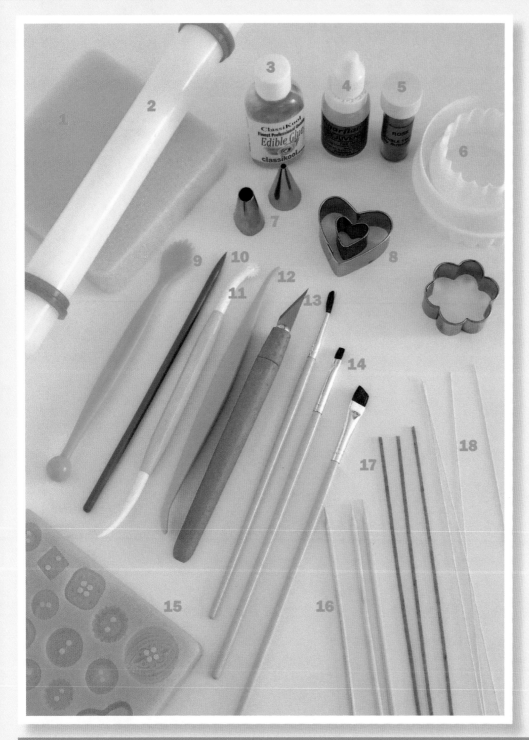

1 **Foam Pad** – holds pieces in place while drying.

2 **Rolling pin** – acrylic works better than wooden when working with fondant/paste.

3 **Edible glue** – essential when creating models. See below.

4 **Rejuvenator spirit** – mix with food colourings to create an edible paint.

5 **Petal Dust, pink** – for adding a 'blush' effect to cheeks.

6 **Round and scalloped cutters** – a modelling essential.

7 **Piping nozzles** – used to shape mouths and indents.

8 **Shaped cutters** – various uses.

9 **Ball tool/serrated tool** – another modelling essential.

10 **Small pointed tool** – used to create details like nostrils and holes.

11 **Quilting tool** – creates a stitched effect.

12 **Veining tool** – for adding details to flowers and models.

13 **Craft knife/scalpel** – everyday essential.

14 **Brushes** – to add finer details to faces.

15 **Moulds** – create detailed paste buttons, fairy wings and lots more.

16 **Wooden skewers** – to support larger models.

17 **Spaghetti strands** – also used for support.

18 **Coated craft wire** – often used in flower making.

## Edible Glue

Whenever we refer to 'glue' in this book, we of course mean 'edible glue'. You can buy bottles of edible glue, which is strong and great for holding larger models together. You can also use a light brushing of water, some royal icing, or make your own edible glue by dissolving ¼ teaspoon tylose powder in 2 tablespoons warm water. Leave until dissolved and stir until smooth. This will keep for up to a week in the refrigerator.

# Making Faces

A veining tool will create indents for features.

The end of a piping nozzle can create a great smile shape.

When adding tiny pieces of fondant for eyes, use a moist fine brush.

Edible pens can be used to draw on simple features.

Pink petal dust adds blush to cheeks.

The faces featured in this book vary in terms of detail and difficulty. If you're a complete beginner, you may opt to use edible pens to draw on simple features. As your confidence grows, you can use fondant for eyes and pupils, edible paint for lashes, or combine the two for some great detailing.

# Adding Hair

A really cute way to personalise any cake is to make the hair on your model to match the birthday girl – and create a mini-me to top her cake! Is she blonde or brunette? Wears pigtails or curls? So many possibilities!

## Side Ponytail

## Cute Pigtails

## Long Hair

When making small figures for cupcakes, it's great to place each on a topper disc, and place this on top of a lovely swirl of buttercream. This way the figure can be removed and kept, and the child can tuck into the main cupcake.

Regular round cutters are essentials, and there are also a great selection of embossing tools and sheets out there that, when pressed into your rolled paste, will create cool quilting effects on your disc. Make your discs first and allow them to harden before you fix your figures to them.

You can also combine a scalloped cutter with the point of a small, round piping nozzle to create discs with cut-out holes.

Plunger cutters are a great way to add cute details to your models. They cut and then 'push' each small piece out, making it easy to cut small flowers, leaves and shapes.

# Creating Frills

Throughout this book we feature lots of pretty frilled dresses and ballerina skirts – here's an easy way to make your fondant or paste 'ruffle' at the edges.

Place on a foam mat, and move the ball tool around the edges, lightly, to frill.

Allow each layer to dry before adding to your cake.

You can also use small pieces of foam to support your frills while they dry.

## Materials

Modelling paste:
Blue
Pink
Yellow
Ivory
Black
Food colour: black
Sugar pearls: white, black
Petal dust: pink
Rejuvenator spirit
Edible glue

## Tools

Craft knife/scalpel
Half styrofoam ball
Toothpicks
Veining tool
Ball tool
Paintbrush x 2
Foam sheet
Soft dusting brushes
Cutters: circles – various sizes, daisy flower

**1** Prepare a half styrofoam ball to be used as the base of the princess dress.

**2** Thinly roll out white paste and cut out a round shape the same size as the base of the styrofoam ball.

**3** Attach the round paste onto the base of the styrofoam ball.

**4** Thinly roll out pale blue paste and cut out 2 pieces of slightly curved rectangle shapes.

**5** Place these pieces onto the foam pad and slightly thin out the bottom edges only.

**6** Gather the top part of each piece to create soft pleats.

**7** Brush the top part of the styrofoam ball with edible glue and attach the paste pleats on to the styrofoam ball.

**8** Thinly roll out white paste and cut out four small circles.

**9** Place the circles onto a foam pad and slightly thin out the edges to create soft ruffles.

**10** Attach them to the top part of the dress. Insert a toothpick half way through the styrofoam ball.

**11** To make the body, roll out pale blue paste into a cylinder shape and flatten it slightly.

**12** Brush the bottom part with edible glue and attach the body by carefully inserting it through the toothpick.

**13** Thinly roll out white paste and cut out a daisy shape using a daisy flower cutter.

**14** Attach the daisy shape onto the back of the dress.

**15** Roll out ivory paste into an oval shape to make the doll's head.

**16** Attach two black sugar pearls to make the eyes and paint the eye lashes.

**17** Thinly roll black paste and cut out a small circle slightly bigger than the head shape, plus shape two pieces into a "comma" shape for pigtails.

**18** Wrap the black circle around the head and shape the fringe. Attach pigtails, and create hair lines using the veining tool. Add in small balls of pink paste.

**19** To make the doll's dress, thinly roll pink paste and cut it into a rectangle shape.

**20** Make small dots using a toothpick on the bottom part of the rectangle only.

**21** Gather the top part of the rectangle and glue the sides together to shape the dress.

**22** To make the doll's arm, legs and shoes, roll out three pieces of ivory paste into long cone shapes. Attach two small pink balls to the ends for shoes.

**23** Roll ivory paste into two thin sausages, slightly bent, and shape hand area and fingers. For the neck and shoulder, make a bottle shape and cut side and bottom with a knife.

**24** Attach the princess' shoulder and the right arm onto her body. Then attach the doll's head and the dress.

**25** Attach the doll's arm and legs. Then attach the princess' left arm.

**26** Dust the doll's cheeks with pink petal dust powder.

**27** Roll out two pieces of white paste into a sausage shape.

**28** Attach them to the princess' shoulder to make the puff sleeves, and mark with veining tool. Let everything dry before attaching the head.

**29** To make the necklace, roll out the paste into a really thin string.

**30** Brush the neck area with a bit of edible glue, attach the necklace on to the neck and attach one ivory sugar pearl in the middle.

**31** To make the princess' head, roll a ball of ivory paste.

**32** Attach it to the princess' body. Shape the mouth using the veining tool and the eyes using the ball tool. Let the head dry completely before attaching the hair.

**33** To make the eyes, roll out really small pieces of black and white fondant.

**34** Because of the tiny size, use a slightly wet brush to pick them up.

**35** Attach them to the face and carefully flatten them slightly using your finger.

**36** To make the hair, roll out black paste and shape it into a round, thick shape. Make sure that it is bigger than the shape of the head.

**37** Attach this to the head and carefully shape it to fit the head.

**38** Using the veining tool, make lines and indentations to create the hair lines and shapes.

**39** To make the pony-tail, roll out black paste into a sausage shape then carefully shape it into a soft wave look.

**40** Attach this to the princess and use the veining tool to create hairlines.

**41** To make the mini ruffle rose, thinly roll out pink paste and cut into a long rectangle shape.

**42** Place this onto a foam pad and slightly thin out the edges to create a soft ruffle.

**43** Carefully roll it into a rose shape.

**44** To make the crown, roll out yellow paste and cut it into a rectangle shape. Then carefully cut a zig-zag shape using a knife.

**45** Attach the sides together to shape the crown.

**46** Attach the crown on the princess' head. Colour the mouth with pink petal dust using a small thin brush. Lastly dust her cheeks with pink petal dust!

# Princess Cupcakes

Once upon a time...

## Materials

**Modelling paste:**
White
Baby blue
Pink
Egg yellow
Green
Purple
Black
Food colour: white
Petal dust: pink
Rejuvenator spirit
Edible glue

## Tools

Craft knife/scalpel
Scallop tool
Veining tool
PME Star cutters
(set of three)
Pastry cutters – round
Paintbrush

**1** Start by cutting some discs in various colours and allow them to dry – these will form the base for each cupcake topper design.

**2** Roll out a thin sausage for the wand handle.

**3** Cut out two stars, one large and one small.

**4** Assemble the wand on the disc.

**5** Paint on some polka dots using the white gel colouring mixed with rejuvenator spirit and fine brush.

**6** Now prepare the green discs for the crown toppers.

**7** Roll out some paste, and cut a long strip. Make zig-zag cuts along the strip.

**8** Moisten one end of the strip and glue together.

**9** Roll out little balls and attach to each of the points on the crown. Secure the crown to a disc using edible glue or water.

**10** Paint little polka dots for added details.

**11** Now choose the colours and discs to use for the mini castles!

**12** Roll out a cylinder with some paste.

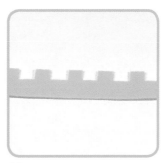

**13** Cut a long strip of paste, and make small cuts to make the crenulations.

**14** Roll out two long cylinders, and make two cone shapes to make the turrets.

**15** Wrap the crenulations shape around the top of the cylinder and place the two turrets at the side of the castle. Add a little door shape, paint on windows, and place castle on disc.

**16** Now for something over the rainbow! Start with a pale blue disc.

**17** Roll four thin sausages of paste in four different rainbow colours.

**18** Arrange them on a disc of sugarpaste in a rainbow shape, leaving room for the cloud on one side.

**19** Roll out various sized white paste balls, sticking them together with a little water as you go.

**20** Cover the balls with a thin layer of white paste, cut around the edge and attach to the end of your rainbow.

**21** Every princess needs some lovely jewels!

**22** Arrange lots of little white balls into a necklace shape on a disc of sugarpaste, leaving room for the main jewel.

**23** Make a teardrop shape.

**24** Score criss-crossed lines with a veining tool.

**25** Attach the jewel to the necklace.

**26** Royal roses!

**27** Roll out a long piece of paste. Start folding the top edge over.

**28** Start rolling the paste into a spiral, turning the top edge over as you roll.

**29** Cut the excess paste off the bottom of the rose, so it sits flat.

**30** Roll out a teardrop shape, flatten slightly, and mark on leaf patterns with a veining tool.

**31** Attach to the sugarpaste disc and paint on some polka dots.

**32** Beautiful Bows!

**33** Cut out the shape in the picture with a craft knife.

**34** Fold the two outside edges into the centre.

**35** Cut a strip and fold across the centre, securing with water. Cut two strips to make the tails, cutting V's at the ends.

**36** Attach to the sugarpaste disc, and paint on some polka dots for detail.

**37** Prince or Frog?

**38** Roll out a teardrop shape for the frog's body.

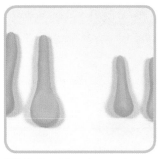

**39** Roll out four tapered sausage shapes, and flatten the larger ends. Make sure the back legs are longer than the front legs.

**40** Attach the legs to the body, bending the back legs at the knee.

**41** Roll out a ball for the head, adding two paste eyes. Repeat steps 7-10 to make a crown. Mark mouth with scallop tool and dust petal dust onto cheeks.

**42** Time for a fairytale!

**43** Roll out some white paste quite thickly, and cut out a rectangle with a craft knife. Along two short and one long edge, mark the page details with a veining tool.

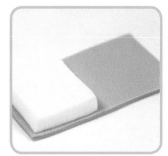

**44** Cut out a rectangle of paste with a craft knife, and lay the book pages on top.

**45** Flip the cover on top of the book, trimming if necessary. Mark the spine using your craft knife.

**46** Attach to a disc, use black colouring and a fine brush to paint the detail on the book, then white polka dots on the disc.

**1** For the body, mould some flesh paste into a teardrop shape. Roll a ball for the head. Insert wooden skewer through the body, leaving space to add the head later. Leave to dry.

**2** Roll two sausage shaped pieces of flesh paste for the legs. Squeeze a little dent to form the knee and then the ankle. Shape the foot area into a soft point.

**3** Gently slide and glue the legs underneath the body. Lightly shape the legs over the side creating a sitting position.

**4** Roll a thin piece of pink paste for the skirt. Trim to the shape shown. Any excess can always be removed when fitting to your model.

**5** Drape the skirt around the body, trimming the excess, then glue in place. Keep the shape a little wide to create a fuller look.

**6** Cut 2 x teardrop shapes from lilac paste for the sides of the gown, trimming a small piece away from the tops.

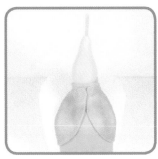

**7** Place a piece on either side of the underskirt, gently tucking underneath. Glue in place.

**8** Roll 4 x thin sausage shapes of lilac paste, long enough to edge the overskirt you have just created. Position and glue two on either side.

**9** For bodice, cut a piece of lilac paste, making a notch in the centre for the neckline. Cut a strip of pink paste for the waistband. Wrap and glue both in place.

**10** Roll 2 flesh paste sausage shapes to form arms. Gently form elbows and wrists then thumb and fingers. For the arm caps, roll a small ball of paste, indent lightly with your ball tool and add detail.

**11** Attach the arm caps and gently insert the arms into the space created by your ball tool. Leave the arms free until you decide how you want your princess to be positioned.

**12** Roll a flat piece of paste (in your chosen hair colour) and use the veining tool to create an indented wave effect. Be careful not to push through the sugarpaste.

**13** Apply the hair in sections, trimming as you go. It helps to create a natural hair parting as your guideline.

**14** Finally add a nose, eyes and mouth. Add accessories such as a crown and wand – see overleaf for details.

# Crown Princess Cupcakes

**1** Cut the required number of 78mm (3in) paste circles and cup these over the foam domes to form. Allow to dry. Cut the required number of smaller paste discs and dry until firm.

**2** Attach the formed sugarpaste domes to your prepared cupcakes using a swirl of buttercream. Leave the smaller discs aside – you will decorate these *before* applying to the cupcake.

**3** Cut a square of sugarpaste, approx. 12mm (½in) thick. This will form the cushion on your cupcake.

**4** Using your fingers, shape the square as shown. Do this all the way around, top to bottom and side to side so that no sharp edges remain and everything is rounded.

**5** Place the shape over the cupcake and gently press down on the corners. Use the leaf tool to create 'folds'. Add little strips of paste to the corners to form tassels, and paint gold, then add tiny hearts.

**6** Cut a piece of paste approx. 70mm x 30mm (1¼ x 2¾in) and using your scalpel or sharp knife, cut little triangles out. This will form the Princess crown.

**7** Carefully bring the ends together, attaching with edible glue. Tease the points slightly outwards and allow to dry.

**8** You can add little balls of paste to the points of the crown and paint everything gold for a regal look! Adding a little heart looks cute too.

**9** Cut a 30mm (1¼in) square of sugarpaste, then roll 2 x contrasting sausage shapes equal in height and trim so that each end is flat.

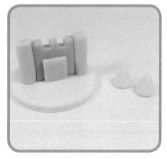

**10** Cut 2 x small notches from the top of the 'castle' and attach to a dried paste disc. Glue the sausage shapes either side. Cut a smaller contrasting square and create two little 'turrets'.

**11** Attach the smaller square and turrets. You can even add a little door if you like!

**12** Paint the turrets and door with gold lustre mixed with rejuvenator spirit. Add 'windows' using an edible ink pen. A little heart can be added too.

**13** To make a wand, cut a star and a narrow strip of paste with a little point at the end. Glue together. Create 'stripes' on the handle with a veining tool.

**14** Again, paint with edible lustre and finish with a little heart.

# Golden Princess

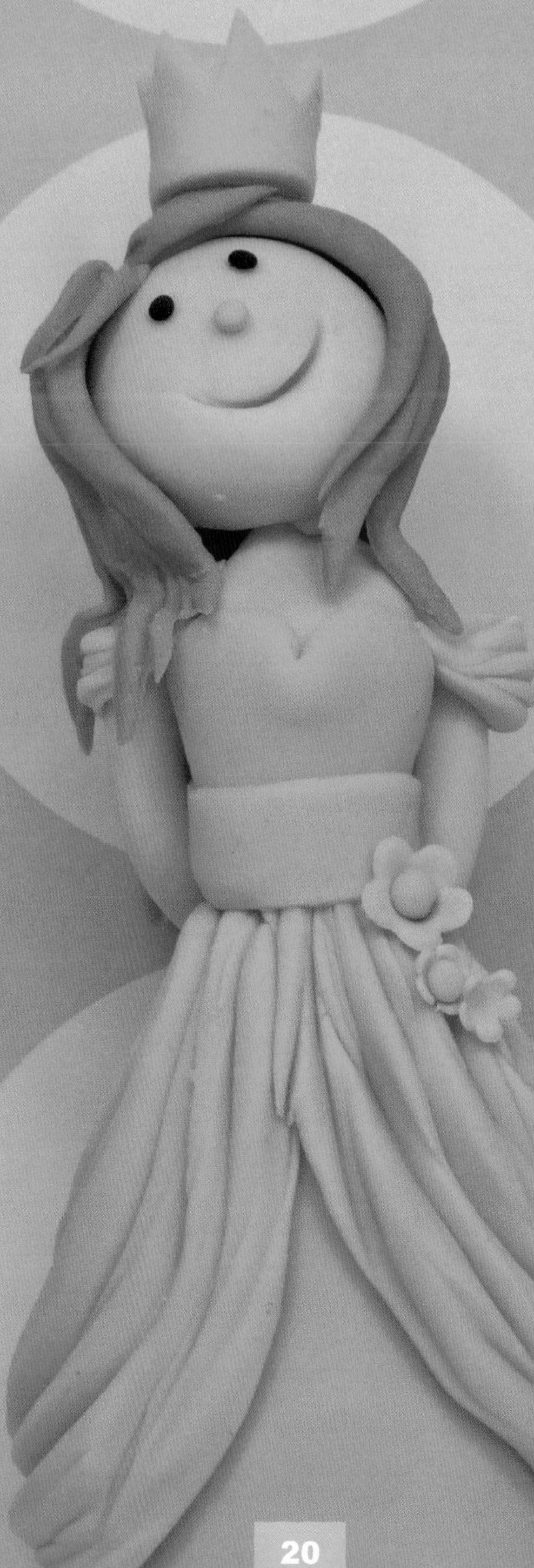

## Materials

**Modelling paste:**

Yellow

Flesh

Hair colour

Pink

Black (pinch)

Black edible pen

Petal dust: pink

Edible glue

## Tools

Craft knife/scalpel

Toothpicks

Spaghetti strands

Veining tool

Quilting tool

Paintbrush

**1** Shape a handful of yellow paste into a cone, for the dress. Insert a spaghetti strand into the top. Leave to dry for 10 minutes.

**2** Roll more yellow paste into two ovals. Lengthen the points and flatten. Texture the paste to represent drapes.

**3** Attach these to the skirt of the princess, meeting at the front. Secure with edible glue.

**4** Shape the body from flesh modelling paste. Start with an egg shape, elongate and thin the waist to match the waist of the skirt.

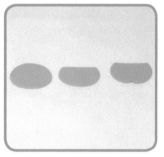

**5** Now roll and cut out a circle, removing a small section to give a flat end. Indent the opposite end with the pointed end of the veining tool to create the bodice.

**6** Attach to the body with the indentation at the front of the dress. Cut a further strip to wrap around the waist as a high belt. Attach with a little edible glue.

**7** Arms: take some flesh paste. Shape into a sausage then shape the wrist and hand. Make tiny sleeves using the same technique as in step 2.

**8** Glue the arms to the body so that she looks like she is standing with her hands behind her back. Attach the sleeves to the bodice, draping over the top of her arms.

**9** Head: roll a head-shaped ball from flesh paste. Add a nose and shape the mouth by using the broad end of a piping nozzle. Add ears and nose.

**10** Place at an angled position so the pose matches with the pose of the hands in an innocent appearance.

**11** Hair: use some paste in the colour of your choice. Take rough oval shapes and add texture, then cut out v shapes at the end of the hair.

**12** Attach to the head with edible glue. Build up the hair with oval shapes for fringe and add eyes.

**13** Crown: roll yellow paste into a ball and flatten. Roll out a thin strip, cutting out the points of the crown. Wrap around the flattened ball. Secure to head.

**14** Complete the dress with three pink blossoms, one large and two small. Glue to dress to finish.

# Rose & Crown Cupcakes

To make a
*simple*
*crown*
See pages
11 & 13

22

## Materials

**Modelling paste:**

Pink

Green

Yellow

Icing and sprinkles

Edible glue

## Tools

Craft knife/scalpel

Coated craft wire

Veining tool

Ball tool

Cutters: leaf shape

**1** This 'roll' technique is the easiest way to make a small fondant or sugarpaste rose! First roll a small amount of pink paste.

**2** Cut into a rectangle, then fold over on the long edge to add thickness to the base of your rose.

**3** Slowly roll up your rectangle and you will see a rose shape forming!

**4** Cut away any excess near the base. Use a cutter, or craft knife and veining tool, to create a couple of green leaf shapes.

**5** Now to try another rose technique. Cut 5 small circles from pink paste.

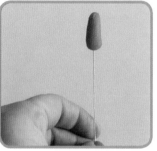

**6** Next create a small cone shape to form the centre of the rose, and squeeze it around a bended piece of coated craft wire or a wooden skewer.

**7** Before you use each paste circle, use the ball tool to soften and ruffle the edges slightly.

**8** Attach the first circle, wrapping it around the centre cone of the rose.

**9** Do the same with the second circle, beginning around the middle of the first circle. Each new circle will slightly overlap the previous one.

**10** Continue with the third circle and you should start to see a rose shape forming.

**11** Repeat with circles 4 and 5, overlapping the previous one and bending out each petal as you go.

**12** There will now be some excess paste at the base of the rose. Cut away.

**13** Your pretty rose is now ready to add to your cupcake.

**14** As in Step 4, create some green leaf shapes. Position the rose and leaves onto iced cupcakes, and add some matching pretty sprinkles.

## Materials

**Modelling paste:**

Flesh

Pink

Yellow

White

**Edible pens:** black, pink

**Petal dust:** pink

**Non-pareils:** white

**Edible glue**

## Tools

Craft knife/scalpel

Cake dummy

Toothpicks

Wooden skewer

Veining tool

Round fluted cutters, various sizes

Heart cutter

Tiny flower cutter

Paintbrush

**1** Using flesh paste, create an hourglass torso shape in the size required for your cake. Insert a wooden skewer through the centre, leaving enough support for the head, and position on a cake dummy.

**2** For the legs, roll 2 x sausage shapes of flesh paste which taper towards the ends. These should be a little longer than the torso length.

**3** Prepare the head by rolling a ball of flesh coloured paste and allow to dry until firm to the touch.

**4** To make the tutu, cut at least 3 large fluted circles of pink paste, more if you want the skirt to be very full. Using a toothpick, roll firmly on each scallop to create a frill. Repeat for each circle.

**5** Cut a smaller circle from the centre of each tutu layer and cut a slit in each one too.

**6** Position the legs on the body, attaching with toothpicks if necessary for support. Arrange the legs in a crossed position, securing with edible glue. Gently shape the knees and feet.

**7** Begin layering the tutu – keep the bottom layer widest and decrease the width with each additional layer. The split in each layer will help with this. Glue as you go.

**8** Use a heart shaped cutter for the bodice (see Pretty Ballerina cupcakes overleaf). Trim to size and attach to body.

**9** For the arms roll 2 x sausage shapes, tapering at one end. Gently pinch to suggest the elbow, wrist and hand. Use your scalpel tool to create fingers and thumb.

**10** Use a small strip of contrasting paste for the waistband. Attach the arms and place into position. Add a small ball of sugarpaste to create a neck and attach head.

**11** Cut 2 x thin circles of yellow sugarpaste and trim approx. ⅓ from one side. Roll a small ball of yellow paste to create the hair 'bun'.

**12** Layer the pieces and attach the bun. Create a 'strand' effect in the hair. Add 2 small balls of flesh paste for ears.

**13** Shoes: cut 2 rectangles of pink paste. Make triangular notches in each. Cut 2 thin strips for 'ribbons'. Make tiny flowers to trim the hair.

**14** Wrap and glue the little shoes and 'ribbons' in place. Attach flowers around the 'bun'. Add her facial features and some petal dust to blush her cheeks.

# Pretty Ballerina Cupcakes

## Materials

Modelling paste:

White/ivory

Pink

Pink/white sugar pearls

Edible glue

## Tools

Craft knife/scalpel

Toothpick

Veining tool

Ball tool

Round fluted cutters, various sizes

Large heart cutter

**1** Cover your cupcakes with ivory fondant or paste. Adding some buttercream beneath will keep them moist.

**2** For the 'tutu' cupcakes, cut 1 x 58mm and 1 x 48mm (2 and 2¼in) fluted circles of pink paste per cake.

**3** Using a toothpick, firmly roll the tip along each scallop to create a ruffle. See page 7.

**4** Once each circle has dried a little, glue them to the cupcake – the larger goes on the bottom, the smaller one on top.

**5** Cut a large sugarpaste heart then remove the bottom part, as pictured. Discard the bottom piece.

**6** Mould the piece into a bodice shape and attach to the 'tutu' using edible glue.

**7** Gently glue a little line of sugar pearls around the waistband of the dress. You may wish to use tweezers at this stage as they can be a little fiddly!

**8** Roll 2 x short sausage shapes from sugarpaste which will form ballet shoes, approx. 40mm (1½in) in length.

**9** Using your ball tool, rub back and forth along the inside of the 'shoe' to create a realistic foot cavity.

**10** Gently bend the shoes in the centre to create an 'en pointe' look.

**11** Use edible glue to fix the shoes to the cupcake, laying one across the other at an angle (pictured).

**12** Cut 4 x thin strips of paste to form the ballet shoe ribbons.

**13** Attach the end of 2 ribbons to rear of each shoe. Bend slightly to suggest movement, trim any excess length and fix in position with edible glue.

**14** Add a tiny bow to complete the look!

## Materials

Modelling paste:

**Lilac**

**White**

**Flesh**

**Sunflower**

**Pink**

**Black**

**Petal dust: pink**

**Small amount of royal icing**

**Edible glue**

## Tools

**Craft knife/scalpel**

**Foam pads**

**Veining tool**

**Cutters: scalloped, round**

**No.2 piping nozzle**

**Small piping bag**

**Paintbrush**

**1** Cover the cupcake with a disc of white fondant, using buttercream or royal icing underneath will stop the cake drying out.

**2** Cut out a scalloped disc and frill it – see page 7. Place on top of the cupcake and secure with dots of royal icing. Use foam pieces to hold the frills until dry.

**3** Repeat with a lilac skirt layer. Place on the foam pad and frill as before. Place on cake and secure and support as before. Pipe little polka dots of royal icing over skirt.

**4** Shape the bodice from lilac paste, shaping the top into a deep 'v' shape for neck section. Insert a spaghetti strand through the bodice to keep it in place.

**5** The neck is shaped from flesh paste. Start with a triangle then soften shape and insert onto the bodice, smoothing and shaping it in place.

**6** Take some flesh paste and shape two arms, thinning the wrist and flattening the hands. Glue to the bodice, placing in position to dry.

**7** Use flesh paste to form the head, ears, nose, mouth. Add two black eyes, and the remaining yellow paste for the hair.

**8** You can adapt the facial features to match your particular birthday girl!

**9** Change the eye colour...

**10** Match in her hair colour...

**11** Whether she is blonde...

**12** Brunette with pigtails...

**13** Or with curls...

**14** Or she is a Ballerina Princess!

# Ballerina Mouse

## Materials

**Modelling paste:**

White

Pink

Black (pinch)

Black edible pen

Petal dust: pink

Rejuvenator spirit

Edible glue

## Tools

Craft knife/scalpel

Spaghetti strands

Veining tool

Ball tool

Cutters: large round, heart, blossom

Paintbrush

**1** You can make your mouse to either sit on the edge of your large cake, or on a covered cupcake.

**2** Shape the legs from white modelling paste. Roll into two cigar shapes, thin the lower end for the lower leg and foot. Bend to shape an ankle and foot. Bend both legs at the knee.

**3** Roll some pink paste and cut two heart shapes. Paint edible glue on the back and attach to the foot, wrapping around to create the ballet shoes.

**4** Position both legs on cake, securing with a strand of spaghetti or edible glue. Cut pink paste strips for the ballet shoe ribbons. Wrap and glue around the legs.

**5** Roll out white paste and cut out a large circle using the circle cutter. Use a ball tool to frill the edges – see page 7. Secure onto the legs with edible glue.

**6** Repeat the previous step with pink paste for the second layer of the skirt.

**7** Take some pink paste, shape into a broad sausage shape and narrow the waist section. Shape the neck by creating a 'v' shape.

**8** Attach this bodice to skirt with edible glue and push a spaghetti strand through the bodice and into the skirts. Add a thin strip for the waistband of the dress.

**9** Cut out a blossom and attach to hide the join of the waistband using edible glue.

**10** With white paste, shape into a triangle for the neck. Fit it into the top of the bodice, securing in place with edible glue and a spaghetti strand, ready for the head.

**11** For the mouse head, roll white paste into a ball, then shape into a teardrop, upturn the pointed end for the nose of the mouse.

**12** Indent the mouth with the scalpel and paint pink. Roll two circles of white paste for ears, attach with edible glue. Draw on the eyes, dust cheeks and add a pink nose.

**13** Shape the arms from white paste. Roll into a cigar shape then narrow to create wrist and hand. Attach to body using edible glue. Support with squares of foam until set in the position you want.

**14** Make a bow headband from strips of pink paste. Fold centrally and add another strip where the ends meet. Attach to the head using edible glue, then attach the head to the body.

# Ballet Shoes

## Materials

**Modelling paste:**

Pink: 180g (6.4oz)approx

**Dusting powder:**

silver (optional)

**Edible glue**

## Tools

**Craft knife/scalpel**

**Quilting tool**

**Veining Tool**

**Wheel cutter**

**Paintbrush**

**1** Roll out approx. 25g (.9oz) pink modelling paste quite thinly – ensuring it is big enough to fit the sole template from p.43.

**2** Cut out the sole of shoe with the scalpel. Cut smoothly –don't drag it– to ensure smooth curves and edges.

**3** Roll out 30g (1oz) paste. Place the upper template over the paste. It is easier to cut the shape out if you score it first then cut out with the template removed.

**4** Following the score lines, cut out the upper with a sharp scalpel.

**5** Neatly paint around the edges of the sole with edible glue, ready to stick the upper onto the sole.

**6** Attach the upper to the sole, working around the edge, pressing the two pieces together. Bring the back pieces together and trim so they meet exactly, securing with edible glue.

**7** Roll out 10g (.35oz) paste, thinly. Cut a strip approximately 5cm x 1cm (2in x .4in), using the wheel cutter, or a ruler and scalpel.

**8** Dampen the back and attach to the top of the shoe, allowing half of the paste to overlap ready to fold over, and ensuring that the positioning of the ribbon on the outside is neat.

**9** Fold over the ribbon strip onto the inside of the shoe, use the quilting tool to run all the way along the edge of the ribbon to texture a 'stitch' line.

**10** Roll out more pink paste to cut out long strips for the ribbons for the ballet shoes. Cut, texture and position them one at a time, before they become too dry.

**11** Texture all the way around the edge of the ribbons using the quilting tool.

**12** Attach the ribbons to the shoes, bending over the end of the ribbon onto the inside of the shoe. Secure, using edible glue.

**13** Cut a very thin strip of pink modelling paste, fold over to create a simple bow.

**14** Attach to the front of each shoe with edible glue, then dust with silver dusting powder to give a sparkling effect, or leave matte if you prefer.

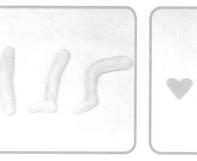

**1** Using flesh paste, shape two legs with feet. See photo; one leg is more bent than the other to get the crossed leg effect.

**2** For the pink shoes, cut two heart shapes, but cut out the central section, then wrap around the foot, securing with edible glue.

**3** Position the legs onto the cake edge, securing with edible glue and a spaghetti strand if necessary. Use slices of foam to support until dry.

**4** Take and roll some white paste, and cut out three scalloped circle shapes and 'frill' the edges (see page 7). Make 3 white and 1 pink.

**5** Place the first skirt over the legs, securing with edible glue. Use slices of foam to support each skirt layer in a fluffed up position until dry. Continue adding skirts, finishing with pink.

**6** Shape the body from pink paste. Make an egg shape, then thin the waist section whilst shaping the neck section into a 'v' shape. Leave to dry.

**7** Shape the neck from flesh paste. Start with a triangle then soften for the shoulders, ensuring it will fit the space at the top of the body.

**8** Attach neck section onto body using edible glue, smooth it so the soft flesh paste meets the body neatly. Attach the body onto the skirts with edible glue and/or a strand of spaghetti.

**9** For the arms: take two pieces of flesh paste and shape into elegant sausages and shape wrist, elbows and hands. Secure onto the body with edible glue and support in position until dry.

**10** Shape some flesh paste into an oval shape for the help, and mark the mouth with the end of the veining tool, and smile edges with a cocktail stick.

**11** Add small balls of flesh paste for the nose and ears. Add the eyes using fondant and black edible pen.

**12** Shape the hair from dark brown paste. Start with a thin, long sausage. Texture with the veining tool and apply to the head using edible glue.

**13** For the pigtail shape use more brown paste and texture, but don't flatten. Glue to head.

**14** Finish the head with two bows made from pink paste – as in the photo. Secure with edible glue, then attach to the pigtails.

## Materials

**Modelling paste:**
**Flesh, Pale pink,**
**Bright pink, Sky blue,**
**Green, Red, Yellow,**
**Brown, Black**
**Edible pens: black, pink**
**Petal dust: pink**
**Non-pareils: white**
**Edible glue**

## Tools

**Craft knife/scalpel**
**Wooden skewers**
**Veining tool**
**Ball tool**
**Cutters: small petal,
flowers**
**Large butterfly cutter
(optional)**
**Paintbrush**

**1** Using flesh paste, create an egg shape which will become the body and a ball shape for the head.

**2** Insert a wooden skewer through the centre of the body, pinch into an hourglass shape. Add a little paste to create a neck. Glue all and allow to dry *before* adding the head.

**3** For the legs, roll 2 sausage shapes, pinching to form the knees and ankles. Slightly flatten for a 'foot' shape.

**4** Shape the leg and foot, as pictured, adding ankle and toe details.

**5** Arrange the legs in a natural seated position and glue the legs to the torso.

**6** Cut a number of varying petal shapes – these will form the skirt. Soften each with your ball tool (see page 7). Allow petals to dry to hold their shape.

**7** Glue the petals to the figure to create a skirt, using the larger size on the base layers, graduating to the smaller size around the waist.

**8** Attach a thin wide strip of contrasting paste to form the bodice, ensuring the seam is at the back. Secure with glue and trim.

**9** For the arms, roll 2 x sausage shapes. Gently pinch to create the elbow and wrist and flatten the hand area. Use your scalpel to create the fingers and thumb.

**10** Arrange the arms in a natural position on your figure and secure with glue.

**11** Roll some brown paste thinly and use your scalpel to cut irregular 'strands' of hair.

**12** Choose a hair parting and randomly add the strands. Work in layers to create a natural look, securing with edible glue as you go.

**13** Continue to build your hairstyle, using shorter strands to create a natural looking 'fringe'.

**14** Add facial features using a tiny ball of paste (nose), and edible pens or paste (eyes and mouth) Accessorise with little flowers and 'fairy wings' (if you have a large butterfly cutter).

# Flower Fairy Cupcakes

## Materials

Modelling paste:
Cream, Pale pink
Bright pink, Sky blue
Green, Red
Yellow, Brown
Black, White
Edible pen: black
Edible glue

## Tools

Craft knife/scalpel
Veining tool
Ball tool
Cutters: flowers
Small paintbrush

**1** To create the toadstools, roll 2 x 'caps' in a bell shape using your thumb and forefinger. Make 2 x smaller 'stalks' in the same way.

**2** Use the ball tool to create a cavity on the underside of the toadstool caps, then veining tool to add texture to the stalks.

**3** Glue the caps to the stalks at slight angles. Stick and press small dots of white paste to the cups to create the spots.

**4** Cut a large leaf shape and 'flute' gently using your ball tool.

**5** Use veining tool to add markings to the leaf then secure on top of cupcake with a little edible glue.

**6** Create a small round 'pad' of red paste and a smaller, jellybean-size piece of black for the ladybug's head.

**7** Glue the two pieces together and use an edible ink pen in black to create the markings (pictured). Secure to the leaf.

**8** Roll 2 x long, thin sausage shapes of contrasting pink sugarpaste.

**9** Twist the two pieces of sugarpaste together...

**10** ...then roll together using the flat of your hand or, for a perfect finish, roll with a cake smoother paddle.

**11** Create the snail's body by making a sausage which tapers at one end. Secure the shell with edible glue.

**12** Cut a small rectangle of green paste and create the 'grass blade' detail with a scalpel tool or sharp knife.

**13** Bend the 'grass' piece slightly and secure to the cupcake. Glue the snail alongside. Add eyes with edible pen.

**14** Create a pretty selection of flowers to add to your cupcakes!

## Materials

**Modelling paste:**

**Flesh**

**White**

**Pink**

**Pale pink**

**Green**

**Black**

**Edible glue**

## Tools

**Craft knife/scalpel**

**Veining tool**

**Cutters: large round**

**Paintbrush**

**1 GREEN FAIRY:** Roll some flesh paste into two sausage shapes. Thin and bend to create the ankle, foot and knee.

**2** Shape a cone shape for body from flesh paste, insert a spaghetti strand for securing the head later. Leave to dry.

**3** Roll then cut green paste into a circle. Trim a little off the bottom and indent the top, wrap around the body and glue.

**4** Cut another circle from green paste and frill the edge (see page 7). Fold in half and place over the legs, secure with glue.

**5** Shape flesh paste into two simple arms, thinning at the wrist and flattening hand section. Glue to attach.

**6** Shape the head from flesh paste, add a nose, ears, eyes and indent the mouth with the end of a cocktail stick.

**7** Using white paste, take 2 pieces and roll into elongated sausages. Flatten, add texture and attach to the head.

**8 PINK FAIRY:** Repeat Step 1 from first fairy and copy the the photo for this fairy's kneeling position.

**9** Shape pink paste into a cone, insert a spaghetti strand into the top for the head.

**10** Take the pale pink paste, roll and cut a large circle. Drape over the body for the dress, then position the legs and glue.

**11** Shape some flesh paste into two simple arms, thinning at the wrist and flattening hand section. Glue to attach.

**12** Shape the head from the remaining flesh paste, adding eyes, ears, nose, indent the mouth.

**13** Roll black paste into a sausage, flatten slightly and texture with veining tool. Attach to head. Add two balls of white paste for bow. Secure head to body.

**14** Cut out two pink wings, texture with a cocktail stick and attach to the back of the body with glue.

# Toadstool House

## Materials

Modelling paste:
White
Ivory
Yellow
Green
Red
Dark brown
Edible glue

## Tools

Craft knife/scalpel
Veining tool
Cutters: circle
Paintbrush

**1** Roll some ivory paste into a cylinder shape approximately 6cms (2.4in) high to make the house. Leave to dry.

**2** Take red paste for the roof. Shape into a flattened cone and create an indentation near top for the roof window.

**3** Roll out white paste and cut a large circle the same size as red roof base. Texture with the pointed end of the veining tool.

**4** Glue the white textured disc to the base of the roof. Texture further with the veining tool to add depth.

**5** Roll some white paste into small balls and flatten. Secure to the roof with glue, then glue the roof to the main body of the house.

**6** For the chimney roll out brown paste and wrap and glue around a strand of spaghetti. Shape more brown into a cone, attach to end and insert chimney into roof.

**7** For the window cut a small oval shape from ivory paste. Add strips of yellow to create the window and glue onto the indentation in the roof.

**8** The roof window is finished by cutting three sections of grass, then securing in place using edible glue.

**9** The house window is made the same way, but with the addition of a window box made from more yellow paste.

**10** For grass at the base of toadstool, roll small teardrop shapes, thinning at one end.

**11** Shape the door and tiny doorknob using brown paste. Score to add texture and glue to house.

**12** Using the same technique as for the chimney, make the stalk of the mini toadstools, using ivory paste.

**13** Form a small red head for the mini toadstool, adding white spots and attaching to the stalk.

**14** Finally shape three mini toadstool roof shapes. Insert ends of the mini toadstools into the house, behind the grass.

RECIPES ♥ TUTORIALS    **Cake & Bake ACADEMY** Est. 2014    RESOURCES ♥ INSPIRATION

**The Cute & Easy Cake Toppers Collection is a fantastic range of mini tutorial books covering a wide range of party themes!**

### Oh Baby!
Cute & Easy Cake Toppers for any Baby Shower, Christening, Birthday or Baby Celebration!

### Princesses, Fairies and Ballerinas!
Cute & Easy Cake Toppers for any Princess Party or Girly Celebration!

### Puppies and Kittens & Pets, Oh My!
Puppies, Kittens, Bunnies, Pets and more!

### Tiny Tea Parties!
Mini Food and Tiny Tea Parties That Look Good Enough To Eat!

## PLUS:

**Passion For Fashion!**
Bags, Shoes, Make-up & more!

**Pirates & Cowboys!**
Ship Ahoy!  Yee-ha!

**Circus Time!**
All The Fun Of The Big Top!

**Vroom Vroom!**
Trains, Planes, Cars, Diggers & more!

**Love, Love, Love!**
The loveliest toppers ever!

**Over The Rainbow!**
A world of rainbow fun!

**Xmas Time!**
Cute & Easy Xmas Cake Toppers!

*and more!*

### Sugar High Presents...
### Cute and Easy CAKE TOPPERS

Brenda Walton and her Sugar High creations are legendary in the cake world. The Cake & Bake Academy bring you Brenda's first ever book! Learn how to make her cute and easy cake topper characters at home.

**A MUST for any cake decorator !**

Printed in Great Britain
by Amazon